Manage to Communicating

Kate Keenan

RAVETTE PUBLISHING

Published by Ravette Publishing Limited
P.O. Box 296
Horsham
West Sussex RH13 8FH
Telephone: (01403) 711443
Fax: (01403) 711554

Series Editor – Anne Tauté
Editor – Catriona Scott

Cover design – Jim Wire
Printing & Binding – Cox & Wyman Ltd.
Production – Oval Projects Ltd.

An Oval Project
produced for Ravette Publishing.

Cover – The amount of attention you give
to transmitting your thoughts determines
whether you communicate purposeful
steam or just hot air.

Acknowledgments:
Angela Summerfield
Barry Tuckwood

Contents

This book is dedicated to
those who would like to manage better
but are too busy to begin.

Communicating

The ability to generate complex thoughts and then to communicate them effectively plays a central part in managing.

Communicating involves all manner of activities: conversing, persuading, teaching, negotiating. To be proficient in any of these, it is essential to understand what communicating is all about and to develop the skills required to be more proficient.

People cannot help but communicate. It is fundamental to human behaviour. But whether you communicate your desire for a bowl of strawberries or your disapproval of something, it is not so much what you communicate but how it is communicated that counts. To be a successful communicator depends on your message being interpreted as credible and appropriate by those on the receiving end.

This book examines the nature of communicating, and gives practical suggestions about how you can get your messages across accurately and cogently so that they are received and understood as you intended.

1. The Need to Communicate Well

Communicating well keeps things moving. When managing, it involves either requesting information or dispensing it, in one form or another; or influencing others to understand and be willing to act upon your wishes.

However, many a problem is caused by inadequate communication or the lack of it altogether which leads inexorably to misinformation and misunderstandings.

Knowing where things can go wrong is a useful starting point when beginning the quest for effective communication.

Signs of Poor Communication

People seldom take enough trouble to express themselves properly. More often than not, this has to do with how something is expressed, rather than with muddled thinking. It is usually easy to detect when people feel something has not been communicated well. They tend to say things like:

- "If you meant that, why didn't you say so?"
- "I wish they'd make it clear what they want."
- "I'm not sure what I'm supposed to be doing."
- "I wish I knew when he/she was joking."
- "I don't really understand."

Often this lack of understanding is not even said out loud. It can simply take the form of a frown or a sigh. From this, it is obvious that what is being communicated and what is received do not always tally. It is essential to find ways of closing the gap.

Not Formulating Messages Correctly

The process by which ideas and information are converted into messages for transmission needs to be properly appreciated. It is all very well to have interesting thoughts and ideas, but there are two things which can prevent good communication:

● The inability to think clearly and logically about what is to be communicated – such as saying "The envelopes are running out" when you mean "We need more envelopes".

● The inability to understand the interests and perceptions of the receiver and to angle the message in order to gain his or her full attention and comprehension – such as using the botanical term 'impatiens' instead of the popular 'Busy Lizzy'.

If the message is not clearly expressed, it cannot be processed properly by others and effective communication cannot take place.

Giving the Wrong Impression

In business people are rarely physically abusive or insulting, but other aspects of their behaviour can inadvertently give an impression that is almost as bad. Three of the worst offenders are:

- **Your appearance**. Lack of care in dressing for the occasion indicates that either you have little interest in those with whom you are communicating or that you wish to dominate them. Distressed jeans and trainers produce quite a different impact from a smart suit. Depending on the situation, either style of dress can give entirely the wrong message.

- **Your terminology**. The use of customary slang used thoughtlessly can offend and distort the message. For example, referring to customers or clients as 'punters' in private might seem to create a feeling of camaraderie, but it indicates an underlying contempt for other people which is unconsciously communicated.

- **Your tardiness**. Not arriving punctually indicates that you consider others to be unimportant. If people are prompt, they are seen to be interested and concerned, but if they are persistently late, it gives others the impression that what has to be communicated cannot be of much consequence.

All these things will communicate that you have not really thought about other people or, if you have, you are not bothered about their views or needs. It is worth thinking about how you can prevent barriers being built before you even open your mouth, by considering how you can create the right impression.

Not Listening Properly

People will tell you they are listening to what you have to say even when they are doing something else, such as reading the paper or doodling. But when they do not do what you asked of them, you are right to suspect that they have not heard you. This is because they have confused listening with hearing.

If people are not listening, they may hear what is being said, but miss something vital because their attention at that moment is elsewhere. Or they only pick up half of the message, while thinking it to be the whole story. The words will have been heard and processed, but not all will reach the conscious mind. For example, if a teacher sees a student is day-dreaming and asks "What did I just say?", the student can repeat a bit of it, parrot-fashion, without comprehension. Or, while someone is talking to you at a party you do not think you are conscious of other people's conversations, yet you will instantly hear the mention of your own name across the room.

If people do not think, from what you say and the way you say it, that you are credible, they are less likely to listen to you. It is not only what you say or write that matters, it is how your message is put across that encourages people to listen to what is being communicated.

It is obvious that when people do not listen to messages or pay attention to what is said, they remember little of them. And if they do not take in properly what is said, there is plenty of scope to get it wrong.

Summary: Managing Communication

Without effective communication, managing is impossible. If you do not communicate clearly, people do not know what you want, what you mean, or what you have in mind. Correct transmission makes the link between thought and action.

Communicating is not something that just happens. It requires attention to the substance of your message and, more importantly, to how it is presented, if it is to get the best chance of being correctly received and understood. Otherwise, you might as well not bother to begin.

Questions to Ask Yourself

Think about how you communicate and answer the following questions:

➤ Do I tend to assume that other people always understand what I am talking about?

➤ Do I fail to think logically and clearly about what I want to communicate?

➤ Do I sometimes neglect to incorporate the interests and needs of other people when endeavouring to gain their attention?

➤ Do I create the wrong impression by not fully appreciating the effect of my behaviour?

➤ Do I sometimes tend to listen only to what I want to hear?

➤ Do I usually leave it up to others to make sense of what I am saying?

If you have answered 'Yes' to some or all of these questions, you may need to examine carefully how you go about communicating.

You Will Be Doing Better If...

★ You acknowledge that people may often misunderstand what you are saying.

★ You determine to think more clearly and logically before communicating.

★ You realize the importance of taking others' interests and needs into account in order to gain their attention.

★ You appreciate that creating the right impression goes a long way to ensuring that what you communicate will get attention.

★ You resolve to take more trouble to listen.

★ You understand the need to get your messages right.

2. Understanding the Communicating Process

In order to understand the communication process, it helps to know a little about how the brain operates. Though it is not yet clear how all of it works, a good deal is known about its activity and how it affects the way people communicate.

Cerebral Processes

The ability to generate complex thoughts and to communicate them is one of the major accomplishments of the human brain. It performs three basic tasks, two of which involve **absorbing** and **processing** incoming data, and a third which is engaged in **generating** it as coherent thought.

Absorbing Impressions

Incoming data that is seen, heard and felt is absorbed and stored by the brain as pictures, words or sounds according to people's unique preferences. For some, visual images make the greatest impact, while for others it can be speech, sounds or touch that matters. These preferred ways of absorbing the millions of impressions being received by the brain on a daily basis are believed to be formed by the age of twelve.

Processing Thought

Different types of incoming data are stored in different 'memory banks' in the brain and, in order to produce thoughts, each has to interact. It is the ability of the brain to retrieve chosen information and make the necessary connections that is important.

It is not easy. There are times when there is no trouble at all but there are times when trying to pull the word out of the verbal bank to name the face stored in the visual bank presents difficulty. It is as if, like the safes in money banks, they have time-locks which are activated by a random time-release switch.

Generating Speech

In order for thoughts to be communicated as speech, a facility for expression has to be generated. This involves labelling objects as nouns, finding verbs and assembling nouns and verbs to form coherent sentences. So, in order to say "The cat sat on the mat", three areas of the brain have to work together.

It is not surprising that people can have difficulties putting what they mean into words. Nor is it surprising if they cannot pick up the correct meaning of something being communicated unless it is conveyed in a form which they can properly understand. Some people need a diagram or a model in order to deal with visual concepts. Many others are able to visualize objects, but cannot find the appropriate label; and some cannot link nouns and verbs together to produce a meaningful sentence. Everyone has experienced times when he or she has had to resort to saying "You know what I mean", in the fervent hope that the other person does.

When there is no appropriate label, one has to be found in order to communicate. An apocryphal tale tells of an early settler in Australia who on seeing a weird-looking animal asked a passing aborigine what it was called. The response was "Kangaroo". What the settler did not realize was that 'kangaroo' meant "I don't know" in Aborigine.

Variable Factors

By and large people's cerebral processes function in a similar way, but to prevent themselves from being overwhelmed by incoming information and stimuli, people learn to pick up and process selectively. This means that:

- Not everything which is disseminated is absorbed.

- What is absorbed will be judged and evaluated in line with each person's individual **perceptual capacities**, **emotional state**, and **sex**.

Your Perceptual Capacities

How people perceive the world plays a vital part in how they generate their thoughts in the first place. Most people are aware that sometimes what is seen is a visual illusion, which plays tricks on the way the brain processes information so that it sees what it wants or expects to see.

Your perceptions are formulated through your basic learning from birth, and include the development of your attitudes and assumptions, your motives and interests. What you perceive will affect how you generate your thoughts in a number of ways, such as when:

- **Selecting information**. People experiencing the same situation rarely take in the same information.

- **Interpreting situations**. People using the same information will almost certainly interpret it in entirely different ways, according to their personal evaluations.

- **Making assumptions**. People interpreting situations may see events or facts as being related when they are unrelated, and vice versa.

Everybody generates thoughts in different and unique ways depending on their impressions, previous experience and expectations. This means that there is plenty of scope for information to be processed in a biased form which in itself affects the communication process.

Your Emotional State

How you feel plays an important part in how you process information and generate thoughts. Long-term and short-term influences are in operation. For example, the effects of an unhappy emotional experience may take some time to get over, and an innocent remark which reminds you of the event may trigger certain feelings which colour your response, possibly to the surprise of others who view the remark as entirely inoffensive. Or an unexpected compliment could increase your confidence and affect what you say, and how you behave, all day.

Your emotional state will filter what information you take in and what you give out. The same message received or transmitted will be treated differently depending on whether you are feeling highly charged or calm and detached. For instance:

● If you are feeling excited or stressed, communication is likely to be hindered because your more rational thinking processes may be clouded by these emotions. You are also likely to receive a message more positively or negatively than was intended.

- If you hold strong opinions about the person communicating with you, your interpretation of the message is likely to be coloured by your view of him or her. Similarly, anything you communicate is likely to be affected by how others view you.

- If you are particularly keyed up about something, you are more likely to pick up only information which is directly relevant to your concern and will tend to ignore or not notice anything else.

So people's emotional states can affect how they receive and transmit messages, and this has a direct effect on how they are received and understood.

Your Sex

Whether you like it or not, your sex plays a part in communication. It is known that the brain structures of men and women differ and that this has a direct bearing on how they communicate. For example:

- In men, the verbal and visual areas appear to be less in touch with each other, while in women there is a greater capacity to integrate visual and verbal information. This means that men are better at concentrating on the particular, whereas women are more able to keep the whole picture in view.

- In men, centres for aggression tend to be more active, while for women it is the emotional centres that have a greater influence. This makes men more competitive and women more collaborative when communicating.

- In men and women, what is said is perceived and received differently. For instance, the simple phrase "I'm sorry" uttered by a man will generally mean, "It's my fault and I take responsibility for it". But the same words said by a woman will usually express sympathy and indicate regret for what has happened. So, if a woman says "I'm sorry" to a man on hearing a tale of woe, the man will often believe that he is being relieved of blame.

So differences which are entirely attributable to sexual identity can significantly influence how men and women absorb and evaluate each other's communications.

Summary: Communicating Systems

Making sure you are communicating properly is always a bit of a lottery, and it is easier to appreciate this if you are aware how people absorb, store and process information, generate thought, and convert that into a system of speech.

But it is also fascinating to consider what happens when people bring to bear their individual preferences.

Then, again, no one person's interpretation can ever be the same as another's. Perceptions, emotions and sexual identity all play a significant part in the way an individual picks up and processes information.

All this not only affects each person differently, but affects them differently from one moment to the next. Communication is in a constant state of flux.

Questions to Ask Yourself

Think about the influences brought to bear on communicating and ask yourself the following questions:

➤ Do I understand that the brain has separate visual and verbal areas from which it has to draw information?

➤ Am I aware that people absorb and process information according to their preferences?

➤ Am I aware that people's preferences influence how they generate thoughts?

➤ Do I understand that people's perceptions influence the way they communicate?

➤ Do I understand that different emotional states will affect the way the people transmit and receive information?

➤ Do I realize that men and women process and communicate information in different ways?

➤ Do I appreciate that communicating is a far more intricate process than I thought?

You Will Be Doing Better If...

★ You understand that there are distinct visual and verbal areas in the brain which require accessing and cross-referencing.

★ You are aware that people have different preferences for absorbing and processing information.

★ You are conscious that people's preferences for what information is absorbed, and in what form, has a direct bearing on the way they think.

★ You realize that people's perceptions influence the way they take in information and impart it.

★ You realize that people's emotional states can affect the way they interpret and remit messages.

★ You recognize that sexual identity plays a significant part in the way people process and communicate information.

★ You appreciate that communicating thoughts is a complex process.

3. Sending and Receiving

Communicating is an active process which involves thought to be transferred and understood by the sending and receiving of messages.

Once a thought has been formed it can stay locked in the brain as a thought forever. This is fine it is what you want, but if you wish to transmit it, it needs to be coded in a form that will clearly communicate to another person what it is you are thinking. No-one can climb into your head to get it out, or browse through your mind as if it were a copy of today's newspaper.

Since communicating is a two-way flow, you need to appreciate both ends of the process of transferring thoughts:

- **Encoding** by the sender – i.e. converting into words the thoughts you wish to convey.

- **Decoding** by receiver – i.e. interpreting the words and making sense of them.

When communicating, you send and receive at one and the same time. The brain has the capacity to process information at four times the speed of hearing speech and so it has plenty of time to prepare a response. But as a sender, you can only know if those at the receiving end are receiving properly when they communicate a reaction.

Sending

No matter what message you are sending, the process needs to be managed and understood. When communicating, you inevitably do two things: firstly, you pass on information and, secondly, and probably more importantly, you form relationships with those receiving the information by creating a favourable impression.

Since what you communicate can range from the simplest fact to a highly complicated concept, how you structure your thoughts makes a difference as to how successfully they are received. This means having to do two things:

- **Marshal thoughts**, which means getting facts and ideas together and putting the key points into a logical order.

- **Transmit information**, which means conveying the right words and images to illustrate your thoughts so that the meaning is clear and the message is suitable.

Marshalling Your Thoughts

Marshalling your thoughts requires concentration. You need to work out the crux of your message and assemble information to support what it is you want to communicate.

Transmitting Information Clearly

Assembling information to formulate your message is one part of the sending process; encoding it, so that you transmit your thoughts accurately, is another.

When deciding what you are going to say, you have to think about the relationship that exists or that you wish to form with your receivers. If you are sensitive to their interests, you will find putting your message together a great deal easier.

The words you choose when transmitting a thought are as important as the thought itself. Words have the power to evoke images, sounds and feelings. They can make the listener feel happy or angry, joyful or sad. You need to use them in such a way that they will convey the meaning you intended, as well as enabling them to be correctly decoded by the receiver.

There are several levels of information you may want to communicate and all need to be appropriately transmitted if people are to understand you properly. For example:

- **Describing Facts**. A salesman is selling you a product. "It's cheap and it's blue," he says. What he has in mind is that it is excellent value and that the colour is known to have a calming effect. But unless he says so, the recipient may not be willing to overcome his or her aversion to the colour blue.

25

- **Giving Opinions**. If these are not flagged as such, a statement like "Arsenal will win the cup", may sound like fact or certain prediction instead of a personal opinion based on utter conviction that Arsenal is the best team in the world. The recipient may feel that there is no leeway for debate.

- **Expressing Feelings**. Saying, "That'll do", as an abbreviated form of appreciation (meaning "You have done an excellent job") is not likely to convey the depth of gratitude felt, or sound sufficiently appreciative, so the recipient may begin to wonder why he or she bothered to make the effort.

- **Indicating Values**. "The money isn't important" might express the attitude that you would far rather enjoy the work than earn a fabulous salary, but someone hearing this could interpret it as meaning you are very wealthy and do not need the money .

Assuming that others will understand your short-hand leads to misunderstandings. You cannot expect people to make a jump in their understanding equivalent to yours. No-one can read your mind and, if you do not express clearly what you wish others to understand, they certainly will not do so.

Sometimes it is necessary to repeat a message before the receiver decodes it correctly. When it is evident that the words you have chosen have not been understood, it is best to restate what you mean in another way, and if necessary, go on doing so until you are sure your message has been received correctly.

Different words and phrases mean different things to different people. By keeping this in mind, you are more likely to choose the words that are the right ones. You will also show the people for whom the message is intended that you are in tune with them.

Using Language Correctly

Language is the filter through which thoughts and experiences are communicated. Often a word can have umpteen meanings, depending on the context in which it is used. For example, 'form': a shape; a species; the bed of a hare; a school class; a document you complete; a bench; or even a criminal record.

Everyone has a range of different types of thoughts and ideas to communicate, from simple statements of fact, such as "The sky is blue", to more complex ones like "I think, therefore I am". But even when people speak a common language, the use of that language is far from uniform. The meanings which people attribute to words may not always reflect the dictionary definition, and much depends upon the way individuals apply the words they use. For instance, people can often:

- Invent words (like 'faxable').

- Inherit words and expressions from their families and friends (such as 'old push face').

- Pick up odd words or catch phrases from others (like 'you know', 'sure', 'loads-a-money').

- Use long words hoping to create an impression (such as 'notwithstanding' instead of 'in spite of').

- Employ jargon (such as 'PC' meaning postcard, politically correct, personal computer or policeman).

Whether you are sending simple or complicated messages, you are also being evaluated by the person receiving them. If you use the conventions of language and grammar properly, people will more readily understand you and correctly interpret what you are saying.

Illustrating Your Point

Many messages are complex and difficult to express in words. Often a diagram can make your point much more forcefully. Indeed, it is said that a picture is worth a thousand words. Some of the most important ideas in the world have been drawn on a tablecloth, blackboard, or the back of an envelope. So, if using an image or story will help people understand or remember the message, never hesitate to do so.

It is worth trying to enliven any dreary facts, like the architect who, having written a mathematical equation on a blackboard, turned to his students and said: "This is the official formula, but all you really need to remember is that a gutter on any roof that you design should be wide enough to accommodate a dead cat."

So, when communicating with others, incorporating a range of pictorial and verbal imagery goes a long way in ensuring there is always a little bit that someone will relate to and remember.

Receiving

Communicating effectively depends upon messages being decoded correctly. However, those on the receiving end will almost certainly be filtering information selectively. There are several reasons for this:

- People take in information in terms of their individual needs.

- People only give attention to the particular aspects of the information that interests them.

- People's perceptions lead them to interpret information subjectively rather than objectively.

- People often read or hear what they expect to see or hear, rather than what is actually there.

This means that what is being received may not always reflect what the sender thinks is being communicated. What is more, if the sender is transmitting filtered information and the receiver is only partially receiving it, a yawning gap can occur which could cause serious misunderstandings.

When decoding (or picking up) a message, various factors affect the accuracy with which you receive the message. Much of this is due to:

- **Judgement**. If you think the person does not know what he or she is talking about, or the source of information is unreliable, you are unlikely to believe it. For example, the report of an event in *The Times* will be considered more credible than the report of the same event in *Pravda*.

- **Bias**. No-one is neutral, so you are more likely to take on board things that you agree with. For example, one politician listening to a diatribe by another who is of a different political persuasion will only hear what he can criticize and will reject the rest.

- **Mood**. If you are feeling depressed, nothing much is likely to cheer you up, and you will turn good news into bad by identifying all the things which could possibly go wrong. But if you are on top of the world, even the worst news never seems all that bad.

All these things can affect the way people receive information and can cause them to pay attention only to specific bits, or to deny that they were given particular facts, even when senders are certain that they have transmitted an accurate message.

Summary: Giving and Getting

There are two key aspects to the communication process. The message needs both to be sent clearly and received clearly. Communicating is the combination of effective sending and effective receiving – a continuous loop.

On this basis, it is the receiver who actually makes the connection; the sender merely speaks or writes, making it possible for the receiver to respond.

A riddle poses the question: 'Is there a sound in the rainforest if a huge tree topples over but there is no-one there to hear it?' The answer is 'No, because unless someone is there to interpret the sound, the communication cannot be said to have taken place'.

Questions to Ask Yourself

Think about sending and receiving information, and ask yourself the following questions:

➤ Do I marshal my thoughts before communicating them?

➤ Do I give due consideration to the words and images I use?

➤ Do I transmit information in a way that clearly conveys the meaning I intend?

➤ Do I always choose words that will be easily understood by those on the receiving end?

➤ Do I make sure I use the conventions of language and grammar to enhance others' understanding?

➤ Do I make an effort to receive messages in a neutral and unbiased way?

➤ Do I appreciate that it is the response of the receiver which indicates that effective communication has taken place?

You Will Be Doing Better If...

★ You marshal your thoughts before communicating them.

★ You consider and choose words and images which will appeal to your audience.

★ You state clearly what you want to say so that people understand what you mean.

★ You know how to use language and grammar to best effect.

★ You try to use appropriate images, tales, parables, humour – *anything* to get your point over to the people with whom you are communicating.

★ You are aware how your interests may affect the way you send messages.

★ You realize that partiality or mood may prevent messages from being accurately received.

★ You understand that communication can only be said to take place when the receiver responds.

4.   Talking and Listening

The secret of communicating well is knowing that **how** you say something is more important than **what** you say. So to create the greatest possible impact you need to use the widest range of expressions available to you through your gestures, your tone of voice and your vocabulary. Research indicates that your voice, tone and appearance account for over 90% of the impression you make on others, as follows:

- **Visual:** 55%. Posture, gestures, the amount of eye contact you use and your general demeanour all contribute to producing an immediate impression. Because your movements and facial expression are deemed to be eight times more powerful than the words you use, you need to be aware of their force and make sure you give them serious attention.

- **Vocal:** 38%. Using your tone of voice, pitch and pace makes a difference to how people interpret what you are saying. Because a third of your impact comes from your vocal delivery, you need to make sure it enhances what you want to communicate.

- **Verbal:** 7%. Your words may not form a large part of your impact but you need to remember that when the effects of visual and vocal wear off, the message is all that remains.

It is clear, therefore, that in order to get your message across and have it fully understood, you need to accompany it with appropriate body language, intonation and emphasis.

Talking

When you talk, you need to imbue your listener with the impression that you are confident and sincere. You do this by demonstrating a consistency between how you present yourself vocally and visually. No matter how brilliant your message, if you are not perceived to be credible by the receiver, it will not be trusted or believed.

Since actions speak louder than words, you need to make sure that they match. Signalling one thing and saying another is construed by people to be a sign of insincerity. If there is a conflict between how you present yourself and what you say (for instance, you are saying "I'm fine", yet your cheek muscles and hands are twitching), people tend to believe your body language rather than the words you use.

Knowing this can help you stay more in control of yourself and enable you to get your message over more effectively. There are several simple things you can do to become more credible and confident and therefore to communicate better. They are:

Using Your Eyes

Looking someone in the eyes (not at their forehead, or over their shoulder) shows that you consider that person to be important. This flatters your listener and prevents his or her attention from wandering, but more importantly, you create your own personal credibility. If someone does not meet your eyes while talking to you, it usually gives you the impression that the person is not interested in what you are saying or perhaps does not like you.

Using Your Face and Hands

All the time you talk, signals are being given – particularly through the face and hands. By using these in a resourceful way you can considerably boost the effect you have on others.

- **Your Face**. Tiny expressions lasting less than a twenty-fifth of a second can reveal feelings which are picked up instantly by others. Smiling makes people see you as approachable. People do not smile as much as they think they do. The genuine smile (as against the fixed grin where the eyes do not reflect the smile) physically changes the chemistry of the brain and makes you feel better. This feeling is instantly communicated.

- **Your Hands**. 'Talking' hands involve listeners and bring them closer to an understanding of what it is you are trying to express. Think about the gestures to which people resort when a foreign language is the stumbling block to communicating. Using open-handed gestures gives a positive emphasis, showing you are enthusiastic and wholly committed to what you are saying.

Visual expressions are part and parcel of your message. If you do not address someone eye to eye, adopt an appropriate expression or use open gestures, people tend not to believe what you are saying.

Using Your Body

While your eye contact and your expressions make a major impact, using the rest of your body can also contribute to the impression you make.

There are various ways your body can indicate how confident you are, which in turn affects the impression you make on others:

- **Posture**. Sitting or standing in a ramrod-like manner can impart authority when this is needed. Slouching the shoulders and crossing the knees may take away from the solemnity of a formal occasion but can make an informal one more friendly.

- **Leakage**. Involuntary movements of the hands and feet can 'leak' a range of emotions from disinterest to anxiety. No matter how still the face and torso, crossed arms, fingers being nibbled or knees jiggled, clearly give away underlying discomfort.

- **Proximity**. Standing too close to someone can create a feeling of invasion or threat. If you stand at a distance of less than 2'-3', your listener will tend to move back instinctively, such is the uneasiness felt when someone encroaches. On the other hand, if you stand 4' or more away, your listener will think you are indifferent and could feel a sense of isolation.

Bodily attitudes lend support to or detract from anything that is being said. You can easily control your own body language by being aware of these things. Enacting one or more gestures to enhance the way you present yourself in different situations will ensure that you reinforce your verbal message with the appropriate visual signals.

Using Your Voice

Your voice is a powerful medium for gaining other people's attention and creating a conducive atmosphere which encourages them to listen.

There are several things to consider:

- **Pitch and Tone**. Lower voices have gravity and tend to be taken more seriously. A shrill or strident voice gives the impression of someone who over-reacts and is not in control. But even the highest pitch has a range from lower to higher, so you can find the lowest level and use it until it becomes natural to do so. Using a modulated tone of voice indicates that you know what you are doing and gives people confidence in you.

- **Pace**. A well-measured tempo keeps attention and enables people to take in the message. If your pace is too fast, they have no time to absorb what you are saying; if it is too slow, you sound lugubrious and boring, so people switch off; and if you are hesitant, people can become unconsciously worried and restless. The natural breathing space enables people to take in what has been said. Constructive use of a pause allows others a moment to reflect and absorb one part of the message before moving on to the next.

- **Emphasis**. Inflection enables emphasis to be placed on certain words. Without sufficient stress, people cannot be sure which are the important bits. On the other hand, if there is too much stress, the listener will very quickly feel punch-drunk and weary and recall little except the fact that it was exhausting.

On the telephone, when there are no visual clues, two things can help to make the best use of your voice. **Standing** straightens the body, which eases your breathing and improves the clarity of your voice. **Smiling** lifts the muscles around your vocal chords, making your voice sound warm and friendly, and acts as a substitute for the missing visual dimension.

Listening

When you listen to someone talking, you need to communicate as much as if you were doing the speaking. You could be listening intently, but unless you indicate that you are, the speaker does not know it.

Without your response in the form of a reaction the speaker cannot assume that you have heard and understood. Showing an interest gives feedback to the speaker and encourages him or her to carry on. Here are some simple and effective ways to indicate that you are listening.

Signalling Your Interest

Signalling that you are interested and involved in what is being said can be done by:

● **Keeping eye contact**. While you listen, you need to look the speaker directly in the eyes. People judge if you are listening to them and absorbing what they are saying by whether or not you are looking at them.

- **Letting speakers have their say**. By allowing others to finish their sentence, and not interjecting, you will demonstrate that you value what is being communicated. People interpret interruption as a lack of respect for their ideas and therefore themselves.

- **Acknowledging**. By nodding and smiling, you acknowledge what is being said and show you are in tune with the speaker. People need to feel that you are giving them a fair hearing.

- **Paying full attention**. By letting go of props (like pencils and keys) with which to scribble, fiddle or fidget, you will cease to create distractions. People interpret doodling, shuffling papers, or clock-watching as not paying attention – even if you are.

- **Relaxing**. By adopting a relaxed stance (such as tilting your head to one side or leaning your weight on one hip), you register your total concentration. People get the impression that what they are saying has your complete attention.

All these signals enable people who are communicating with you to gauge whether or not you are actually listening to and absorbing what they have to say.

Checking Your Comprehension

Checking that you have been listening properly and have heard the message correctly (particularly over the telephone) is done by:

- **Paraphrasing the message.** By restating in your own words what you have heard, you can make sure you have accurately received the message.

- **Asking Questions.** By querying, you test your understanding of the message and also let the speaker know you have been actively listening.

These two-way activities not only ensure you get the right information but also enable the person talking to focus properly on what he or she was really trying to communicate.

Summary: Speaking and Hearing

Whether talking or listening, your gestures, posture, expressions and intonation are fundamental to convincing and comprehensive communication. By using your voice and body to animate what you are saying, you make the maximum impression on your listener. And by actively indicating that you are convinced and do comprehend the message, you create the optimum impression on the sender.

Questions to Ask Yourself

Think about talking and listening and answer the following questions:

➤ Do I fully comprehend the huge impact the visual aspect has on the effectiveness of my communication?

➤ Do I understand that my body language must match my words if I am to be believed?

➤ Do I recognize the power of eye contact in establishing my personal credibility?

➤ Do I understand how I can use my voice to ensure my message is delivered confidently ?

➤ Do I appreciate that I need to let people know I am listening by keeping eye contact?

➤ Do I ask questions to ensure that I have fully understood what is being communicated?

➤ Do I realize that listening is an active process which requires effort on my part?

You Will Be Doing Better If...

★ You understand the major impact your gestures and expressions make.

★ You make sure your body language matches your verbal message.

★ You maintain eye contact when communicating.

★ You use your tone of voice to ensure that people find it interesting to listen to you.

★ You let people know you are listening by looking at them and acknowledging what they are saying.

★ You ask questions to check you have fully understood what is being communicated.

★ You listen actively to what people have to tell you.

5. **Writing and Reading**

Writing things down ensures that there is a permanent record of what it is you want to communicate. But writing is not always easy. There is a golden rule to remember: start by getting it written, rather than getting it right.

Once it is written, you can work on your draft to ensure that it reflects what you really want to say. If you expect to be able to get your thoughts on to paper perfectly first time, you will probably never get started.

Writing Versus Speaking

Writing may take longer and be a more demanding form of communication, but it has a considerable number of advantages over the spoken form.

Written information allows quite complex material to be structured in such a way that it makes sense very simply, and it and enables people to refer to it long after the event.

If you have to communicate something to different people on different occasions, your performance will never be the same. Even a minor addition or omission may make a difference when various people compare what they have been told, whereas with a written message everyone gets exactly the same information.

On the other hand, if the words have not been chosen carefully enough, there is plenty of opportunity for people to misinterpret what is written. You cannot ask a document what is meant by a word or a phrase as you can a speaker, so anything which is not entirely clear can be subject to debate as to its interpretation.

Reading

When people read a document, their overall goal is to find out what it contains and understand its content.

Reading involves making a selective search for information using existing knowledge. To ensure that people find it easy to read what you have written you need to pay attention to:

- The principles of language you use, such as grammar and syntax, metaphors and similes.

- The amount of knowledge the reader may already possess about the subject. People usually know a little about what they read, otherwise it would not be of interest to them.

- The reason the document is being read; for example, whether it is for pleasure or a business requirement.

To read fluently means keeping up a minimum speed which is determined by how easy it is to spot what is coming next. Unfamiliar content or style slows down the speed of reading and if speed is lost, people usually become less interested and may ultimately stop reading altogether.

Simple Rules for Getting it Right

Ensuring that people take on board the specific points you want to convey means arranging your information clearly and concisely. If a message is ambiguous, people can misinterpret what they read and act on erroneous assumptions: they may, quite literally, 'read between the lines'. Clarity and concision usually take extra time and effort – which is the truth alluded to in the old joke "PS: I'm sorry this letter is such a long one, but I haven't found the time to write a short one".

The skill of communicating on paper is to get people to want to read the document. This means:

- **Getting it written, then getting it right**. That is to say, getting it down in any shape, and then taking time to polish and re-phrase what you wish to impart.

- **Using space, headings, paragraphs and indentations**. These are effective substitutes for visual and vocal signals. They provide the emphasis, interest and stimulus which encourage people to absorb written matter more readily and prevent them from getting mentally overloaded, and bogged down.

- **Having headlines and different sizes of typeface** (and even a short synopsis). These act as signposts and make it easier to find your way around.

The language used when speaking is usually free-flowing. Yet people often tie themselves in knots when committing thoughts to paper. For some reason they feel that because they are writing, they need to use words like 'finance' instead of 'pay for', 'manufacture' instead of 'make', 'participate' instead of 'take part', 'however' instead of 'but', and so on. This not only stultifies the message, but often acts as a blockage for the person reading it.

The rule to remember is that simple is best.

Summary: Putting it on Paper

Communicating in writing requires you to keep your reader in mind at all times. Good presentation helps enormously to make written matter easier to follow, and when people can understand what is written they are motivated to carry on reading.

By making what you write simple and approachable, you keep the reader's interest, and leave him or her with the impression that what you wrote was worth reading. It is also more likely to be read a second time.

Questions to Ask Yourself

Think about your written communications and answer the following questions:

➤ Do I take the trouble to write what should be written?

➤ Do I go over what I have written a number of times to get it right?

➤ Do I make sure that things I have written are clear and concise?

➤ Do I lay out my written communication in a way that is easy to follow?

➤ Do I make sure there are enough headlines and variations of display to direct the reader?

➤ Do I use the simplest possible language to express what I mean?

You Will Be Doing Better If...

★ You understand the advantages of writing things down.

★ You first get things written and then work at getting them right.

★ You appreciate that reading involves searching selectively for information.

★ You lay out documents so they make the most impact.

★ You use the right level of language so that people find your documents easy to understand.

★ You avoid using complicated words and phrases, when simple ones express things better.

★ You aim to make your written communication worth reading.

6.   Valuing People

To communicate effectively, you need to have people 'with' you because, in most situations, if they are not with you, they are either neutral or against you.

You may think that in many situations you are only giving people the facts. But to get them to believe what you have to say, consider why are you communicating with them in the first place.

Whatever you have to communicate, you want people to take notice of what you have to say and to think it is worth hearing or reading. To do this, you need to indicate to others that you value them.

Making People Feel Important

You will communicate far more effectively if you indicate that you consider people are the most important part of the communication. You can demonstrate this by:

- **Never contradicting others**. People may hold different opinions from you and if you acknowledge that their opinions are valid, rather than telling them you think they are wrong, you are more likely to get them to listen to your views. "How interesting that you should think that."

- **Accommodating others' ideas**. If you are tolerant of views that are different from yours, people feel their opinions are worth airing and hearing. By showing you have understood what concerns them, you indicate that you see things from their point of view. The more you can accommodate people's opinions, the more you indicate you value them.

- **Not talking over someone or interrupting**. When you want to make a point, the temptation to jump in can be overwhelming. But if you do so, you give the impression that you do not consider the other person worth listening to. By making a mental log of what you want to say (or, in meetings, jotting down a key word), you can make sure you hang on to your point in order to impart it at the appropriate moment.

If you make an effort to treat people in a way which indicates that you think their views are of substance, they will feel valued and will be more likely to value you.

Getting People to Like You

If you can make people think that you have an affinity with them, they are far more disposed to like you.

In practical terms, this can be achieved by:

- **Encouraging people to talk about themselves**. This enables you to obtain information you can refer to later. "What do *you* think about...?" By asking questions and listening to (and remembering) the answers, you make people feel their lives are significant to you. By mentioning salient points when you next meet, you show you care about them.

- **Showing genuine interest**. By asking pertinent questions, you create rapport. "What makes you think that?" By taking notice of other people's preferences and establishing common ground, you show your involvement with them. "I know this is something you feel strongly about..."

- **Using a person's name**. When talking to someone, saying "John/Jane..." gives a personal touch to your communications. People's names are an integral part of their personality and by using them you indicate your interest in them as individuals. This not only makes people feel that they count, it makes them warm towards you.

Taking account of other people's concerns makes them open up to you and consider you worth listening to. If you are prepared to concentrate on the way they think and feel, and on what matters to them, they will relate to you and become more receptive.

Summary: Believing That People Matter

Being interested in other people is an essential ingredient of good communication. If you take the trouble to show that you think they are important, by concentrating on what they are saying and appearing to appreciate it, it will make them feel that they are important, and you will have an open sesame to their minds.

When you believe that others matter you will communicate your belief, and this makes them feel more worthwhile themselves. It also means they are more likely to reciprocate. When this happens, communication can be considered to be at its very best.

Questions to Ask Yourself

Think about your communications with people and answer the following questions:

➤ Do I consider people the most important part of the communication process?

➤ Do I refrain from contradicting people?

➤ Do I tolerate views that are different from my own?

➤ Do I let others finish what they are saying before jumping in with my views?

➤ Do I give them my full attention while they are talking?

➤ Do I ask relevant questions to show my interest in what they are saying?

➤ Do I make a point of using people's names when talking to them?

➤ Do I understand that valuing people's opinions makes for better communication?

You Will Be Doing Better If...

★ You consider other people to be the most important part of communicating.

★ You try not to contradict people.

★ You listen carefully to what they have to say to you.

★ You let others finish speaking before your make your point.

★ You give them your full attention when they are talking.

★ You ask questions of people to show that you are interested in them and what they have to say.

★ You use people's names when talking to them.

★ You value their thoughts and ideas.

Check List for Communicating

If you are finding that you are not communicating well enough, think about whether it is because you have failed to take account of one or more of the following aspects:

Sending and Receiving

If people do not understand what you are communicating, it could be that you have not constructed your message so that it was received as you intended. If you have not presented your information clearly enough or chosen your words carefully, people may find it difficult to follow your train of thought. You may be wasting all your efforts if you fail to understand that it is how your message is received that determines whether communication has taken place.

Talking

If people do not appear to believe what you have to say or seem to be bored, you may have underestimated how much your expressions and gestures need to reflect and enhance what you say. It could be that you have failed to take into account your visual and vocal impact. To be perceived as a credible communicator, you need to pay as much attention to your movements and tone of voice as the language you use.

Listening

If you have not understood what someone has been saying, it may be that your mind was on something else and missed a point. If you do not make the effort to listen actively, you will almost certainly pick up the wrong message. Concentrating on what the speaker is saying, asking questions, and signalling clearly that you are interested in what is being said ensures that two-way communication takes place.

Writing and Reading

If you find that what you have written is often misinterpreted or that people miss the point you want to make, it could be that your use of language is not appropriate for your readers. Or it may be that you have not laid out the document so that people find it easy to read and understand.

Valuing People

If people do not respond to what you have to say, it may be that you are not focussing on them or indicating that you consider them important. You can easily rectify this by eliciting others' points of view and appreciating their ideas. Once you show that you are interested in and value others, better communication can follow.

The Benefits of Communicating Well

Communicating is the central process by which people are informed and guided to perform better. To do it well means not only marshalling your thoughts and presenting them in a way that people will readily understand, but putting them across in a way that motivates people to pay attention.

The benefits of communicating well are:

- You gain greater co-operation.

- You have fewer misunderstandings.

- You find people are more responsive.

- You are seen as someone worth listening to.

- You become more methodical.

- You increase your ability to think clearly.

- You feel more in command of what you are doing.

Communicating well is a two-way process which depends on capturing the attention of others and correctly interpreting what others convey to you. The impression you create is the catalyst to your message and, just as yeast makes dough rise, it is the vital ingredient in communicating.

Glossary

Here are some definitions of words used in relation to Communicating.

Bias – The inclination to prejudice.

Brain – The most sophisticated computer in the universe; only as good as the end user.

Communicating – Expressing yourself in the most effective way.

Emotion – Strong feeling which affects communication for better or worse.

Gestures – Movements which convince the listener that you know what you are talking about, and the talker that you are listening.

Grammar – Elementary rules by which language is made more intelligible, but not necessarily more intelligent.

Language – A method of expressing thoughts by means of words. Getting the right ones in the right order is the tricky bit.

Listening – Actually paying attention to what is being said.

Message – What you need to transmit. Getting it across as you intended is what communication is all about.

Misunderstanding – Failing to make the proper connections. Understandable, given the difficulties.

Perception – Intuitive awareness; usually overlaid by preferences and previous experiences.

Receiving – The task of converting information into something meaningful.

Response – The required reaction to communication, without which you cannot gauge its effect.

Sending – The task of conveying information to a given destination.

Talking – Expressing considered thoughts or, more commonly, unconsidered ones.

Understanding – Interpreting correctly, sometimes in spite of what is being communicated.

The Author

Kate Keenan is a Chartered Occupational Psychologist with degrees in affiliated subjects (B.Sc., M.Phil.) and a number of qualifications in others.

She founded Keenan Research, an industrial psychology consultancy, in 1978. The work of the consultancy is fundamentally concerned with helping people to achieve their potential and make a better job of their management.

By devising work programmes for companies she enables them to target and remedy their managerial problems – from personnel selection and individual assessment to team building and attitude surveys. She believes in giving priority to training the managers to institute their own programmes, so that their company resources are developed and expanded.

Knowing she is expected to communicate clearly and credibly means that she has a thorough understanding of the likelihood of getting it wrong.

She finds that expressing her thoughts through speech is relatively easy, but getting them in the right order to convey the right written message is another matter altogether. Happily, to judge by the general response, she seems to get most of both right.

THE MANAGEMENT GUIDES

Available now:

	Book £2.99	Tape £4.99
Communicating	☐	
Delegating	☐	
Making Time*	☐	☐
Managing*	☐	☐
Managing Yourself*	☐	☐
Motivating*	☐	☐
Negotiating	☐	
Planning*	☐	☐
Running Meetings	☐	
Selecting People*	☐	☐
Solving Problems	☐	
Understanding Behaviour	☐	

These books are available at your local bookshop or newsagent, or can be ordered direct. Prices and availability are subject to change without notice. Just tick the titles you require and send a cheque or postal order for the value of the book to:

B.B.C.S., P.O. Box 941, HULL HU1 3VQ (24 hour Telephone Credit Card Line: 01482 224626), and add for postage & packing:

UK (& BFPO) Orders: £1.00 for the first book & 50p for each extra book up to a maximum of £2.50. Overseas (& Eire) Orders: £2.00 for the first book, £1.00 for the second & 50p for each additional book.

*These books are also available on audio tape by sending a cheque or postal order for the value of the tape to: Sound ƒX, The Granary, Shillinglee Park, Chiddingfold, Surrey GU8 4TA (Telephone: 01428 654623; Fax: 01428 707262), and add for postage & packing the same amount as specified for book postage above.